INSECTS UP CLOSE

Fireflies

by Christina Leaf

BELLWETHER MEDIA • MINNEAPOLIS, MN

Note to Librarians, Teachers, and Parents:

Blastoff! Readers are carefully developed by literacy experts and combine standards-based content with developmentally appropriate text.

Level 1 provides the most support through repetition of high-frequency words, light text, predictable sentence patterns, and strong visual support.

Level 2 offers early readers a bit more challenge through varied simple sentences, increased text load, and less repetition of high-frequency words.

Level 3 advances early-fluent readers toward fluency through increased text and concept load, less reliance on visuals, longer sentences, and more literary language.

Level 4 builds reading stamina by providing more text per page, increased use of punctuation, greater variation in sentence patterns, and increasingly challenging vocabulary.

Level 5 encourages children to move from "learning to read" to "reading to learn" by providing even more text, varied writing styles, and less familiar topics.

Whichever book is right for your reader, Blastoff! Readers are the perfect books to build confidence and encourage a love of reading that will last a lifetime!

This edition first published in 2018 by Bellwether Media, Inc.

No part of this publication may be reproduced in whole or in part without written permission of the publisher. For information regarding permission, write to Bellwether Media, Inc., Attention: Permissions Department, 5357 Penn Avenue South, Minneapolis, MN 55419.

Library of Congress Cataloging-in-Publication Data

Names: Leaf, Christina.
Title: Fireflies / by Christina Leaf.
Description: Minneapolis, MN : Bellwether Media, Inc., 2018. | Series:
   Blastoff! Readers. Insects Up Close | Audience: Age 5-8. | Audience: K to
   grade 3. | Includes bibliographical references and index.
Identifiers: LCCN 2016057234 (print) | LCCN 2017009506 (ebook) | ISBN
   9781626176645 (hardcover : alk. paper) | ISBN 9781681033945 (ebook)
Subjects: LCSH: Fireflies–Juvenile literature.
Classification: LCC QL596.L28 L43 2018 (print) | LCC QL596.L28 (ebook) | DDC
   595.76/44–dc23
LC record available at https://lccn.loc.gov/2016057234

Editor: Christina Leighton   Designer: Maggie Rosier

Printed in the United States of America, North Mankato, MN.

Table of Contents

What Are Fireflies?

What was that flash? It is a firefly! Many of these **beetles** light up.

Fireflies are also called lightning bugs. These insects have special parts on their **abdomens** that make light.

abdomen

light

ACTUAL SIZE:

common eastern firefly

abdomen

light

ACTUAL SIZE:

common eastern firefly

Fireflies are dark
with red, orange,
or yellow markings.

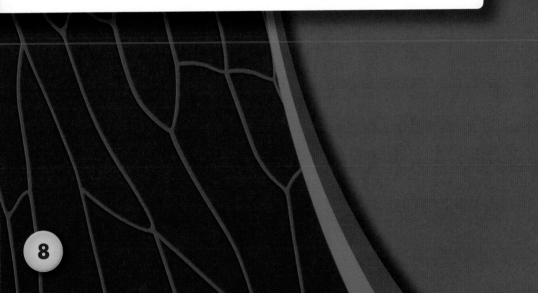

9

Most fireflies have four wings. Leathery outer wings cover thin inner wings.

outer wing

inner wing

Night Lights

Fireflies like forests and fields. They usually shine on summer nights.

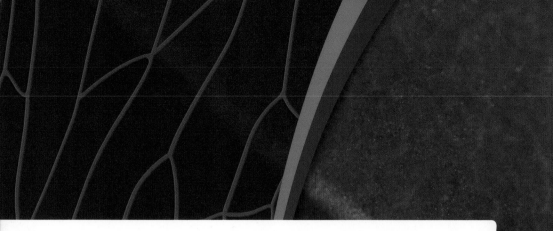

Males and females blink their lights to talk. Each kind of firefly has a special pattern.

Most adult fireflies eat **nectar** or pollen. Some eat other fireflies. Others do not eat.

FAVORITE FOOD:

nectar

Growing Up

Baby fireflies are called **larvae**. They break out of eggs.

FIREFLY LIFE SPAN:
about 2 months

larva

eggs

Larvae turn into **pupae**. Then they become adults. Shine on, firefly!

**adult
firefly**

pupa

Glossary

abdomens

the back parts of insect bodies

nectar

a sweet liquid that comes from plants, especially flowers

beetles

insects with hard outer wings that cover inner flying wings

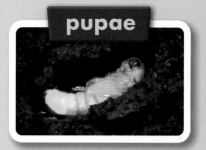

pupae

young insects that are about to become adults

larvae

baby insects that have come from eggs; larvae look like worms.

To Learn More

AT THE LIBRARY

Frost, Helen, and Rick Lieder. *Among a Thousand Fireflies.* Somerville, Mass.: Candlewick Press, 2016.

Morgan, Emily. *Next Time You See a Firefly.* Arlington, Va.: National Science Teachers Association, 2013.

Stewart, Melissa. *Zoom in on Fireflies.* Berkeley Heights, N.J.: Enslow Publishers, 2014.

ON THE WEB
Learning more about fireflies is as easy as 1, 2, 3.

1. Go to www.factsurfer.com.

2. Enter "fireflies" into the search box.

3. Click the "Surf" button and you will see a list of related web sites.

With factsurfer.com, finding more information is just a click away.

Index

The images in this book are reproduced through the courtesy of: Brandon Alms/ Stocksy, front cover, pp. 4-5, 22 (center left); blickwinkel/ Hecker/ Alamy, pp. 6-7; Tyler Fox, pp. 8-9; terry priest/ Flickr, pp. 10-11; NaturePL/ SuperStock, pp. 12-13, 13; kororokerokero, pp. 14-15; Courtney A Denning, pp. 16-17; Srijira Ruechapaisarnnanak, pp. 17, 22 (top right); PREAU Louis-Marie/ Hemis.fr/ SuperStock, pp. 18-19; Andrew Darrington/ Alamy, p. 19; Paulo Oliveira/ Alamy, pp. 20-21; Kazuo Unno/ Minden Pictures, pp. 21, 22 (bottom right); Brandon Alms, p. 22 (top left); prajit48, p. 22 (bottom left).